Boxes
for
God

By God and Jeannette Sabatini

ISBN: 0692420290
ISBN-13: 978-0-692-42029-4 (nettesfeathers)

All verses come, with thanks, from the Easy-to-Read Version (ERV) of the Bible.

Dedication

This book is dedicated to its true author: God! He orchestrated the experiences behind it, provided the words for it, and made the awesome suggestion to add kid-friendly verses.

It also is dedicated to children. May they put their faith in God so they will grow into teenagers and, then, adults who are at peace.

Thank you, God, for allowing me to write down your words and to share this fantastic message!

I have a shelf with boxes for God.

It's in my head, which you may think odd.

Inside the boxes, you won't find things.
Instead you'll find problems that every day brings.

I'm bullied

I'm tired

I'm lonely

When something is wrong, I go to my shelf.
I know I don't have to solve problems myself.
I take down a box and put in my worry.
I give it to God with a request to please hurry.
I know God would rather I enjoy my day.
I tell Him I trust Him each time that I pray.

Give your worries to the Lord, and He will care for you.

He will never let those who are good be defeated.

Psalm 55: 22

Give all your worries
to Him,
because He cares for you.
1 Peter 5:7

I'm teased

For God

When I give God a box, He's very pleased.
Like when I was sad because I was teased.

He will cover you like a bird spreading its wings over its babies.
You can trust Him to surround and protect you like a shield.
Psalm 91:4

He gave me safe shelter under his wings.
I now have the peace that His love brings.

Dean

For God

I gave him the box that I labeled "Dean."
Dean called me names and he always was mean.
God saw the label and I felt His advice.
"Pray for that person and try hard to be nice."

But I tell you, love your enemies. Pray for those who treat you badly.
Matthew 5:44

I'm sure you'll agree that that's hard to do.
Especially when someone's so rotten to you!

But, really, I did it. I prayed hard for that kid.
I'm just so amazed at what our God did!

I will stand like a guard and watch.

I will wait to see what the Lord will say to me.

I will wait and learn how He answers my questions.

Habakkuk 2:1

It took many years... in fact, two or three.
God opened Dean's eyes and he got to know me.

God, You give true peace to people who depend on You,
to those who trust in You.

Isaiah 26:3

I have many boxes chock-full of fear.
Things for which I have shed many a tear.

Where God's love is, there is no fear,
because God's perfect love
takes away fear.

1 John 4:18

I reach for a box
                when fear makes me cry.

The Bible says God
                rules both earth and sky.

He told me He's with me
                wherever I go.

Now I always remember
                that He runs the show.

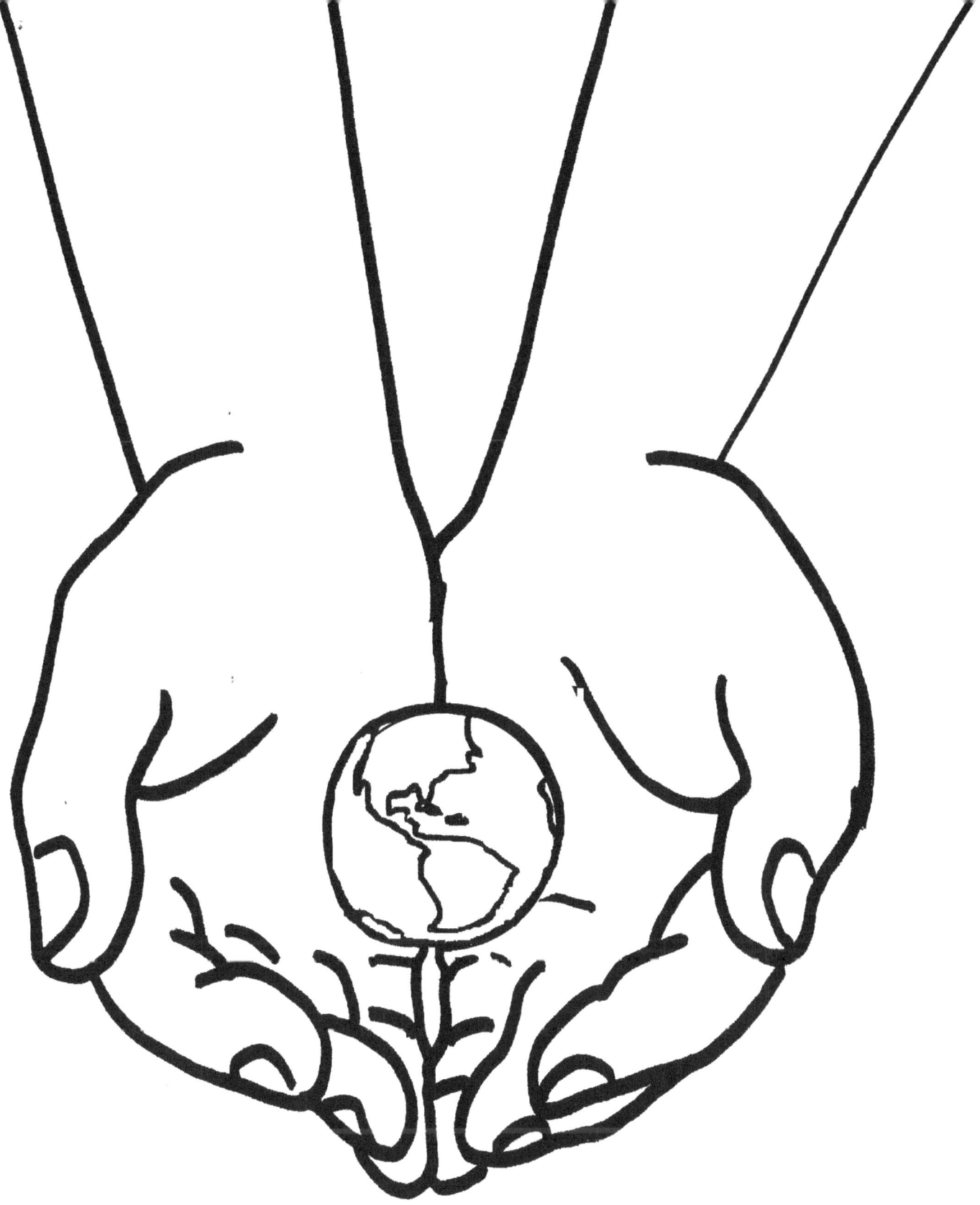

So, give God your box...

He'll know what to do.

He's big and loving...

no problem is new!

He may answer that day,

though it may take a few...

Yet, as you await,

His peace will fill you!

His peace makes it easier

to handle the pain.

It still may be there,

but it won't hurt the same.

What are some of your worries?

Write them on these boxes and then give them to God with a prayer.

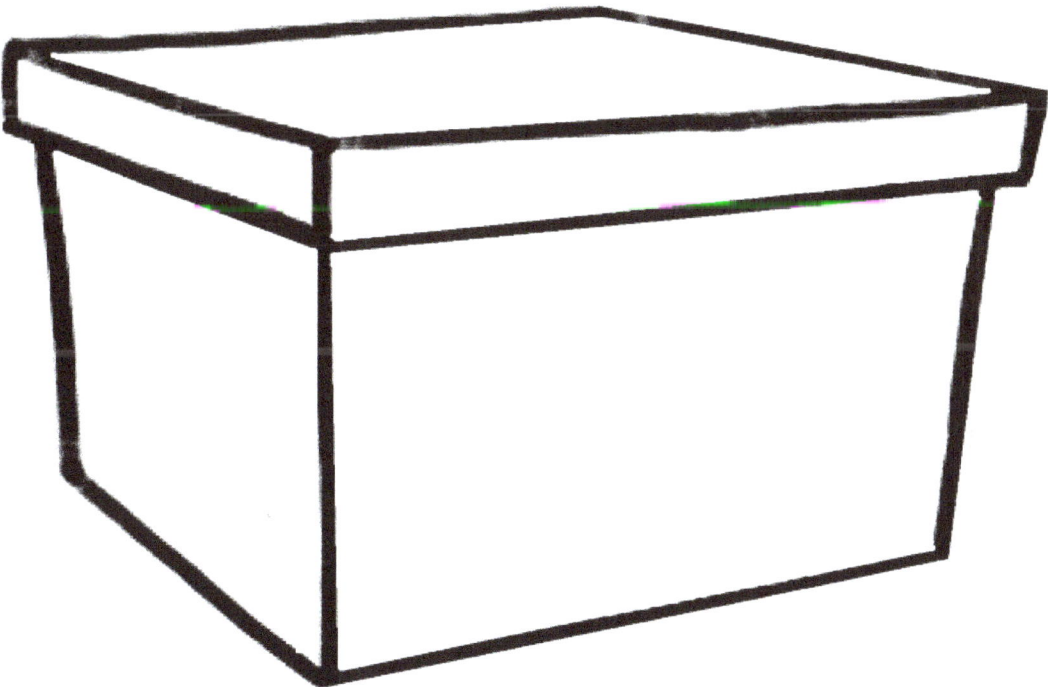

He will command His angels to protect you wherever you go.
Their hands will catch you so that you will not hit your foot on a rock.
You will have power to trample on lions and poisonous snakes.
The Lord says, "If someone trusts Me, I will save them.
I will protect My followers who call to Me for help.
When My followers call to Me, I will answer them.
I will be with them when they are in trouble.
I will rescue them and honor them.
I will give My followers a long life
and show them My power to save."
Psalm 91:11-16

God has said,
"I will never leave you;
I will never run away from you."
Hebrews 13:5

About the Author

Jeannette Sabatini, who holds a degree in English/Journalism, has written and illustrated a number of faith-based and secular books that she plans to release under her Have a Bully-Free Day! title. She also freelances in the medical writing and editing field and works as an aide at an elementary school, a job she loves.

Jeannette just released a book of skits for children's ministry entitled God's Way to Have a Bully-Free Day! Children relate to the skits in this book because they focus on bullying and friendship issues they face every day; each skit demonstrates how problems can be resolved in a Godly way. They are easy to perform and perfect for children to share with other children and/or teens to perform for kids during youth group meetings, Sunday School and Vacation Bible School.

Jeannette thanks her husband, sons, and entire family for their love and support.

www.ingramcontent.com/pod-product-compliance
Lightning Source LLC
Chambersburg PA
CBHW080537030426
42337CB00023B/4781